The Hidden Life of the
DESERT

Photographs and Text by
THOMAS WIEWANDT, Ph.D.
Dwight Kuhn, Series Editor

CROWN PUBLISHERS, INC.   NEW YORK

ACKNOWLEDGMENTS:

The author wishes to thank the many individuals who, over the years, have shared their expertise, advice, and experiences: all have helped to make this a better book. Those who read early versions of the text and offered many helpful suggestions are

Educational Consultants:

Audrey W. Ives, Continental School District, Continental, Arizona
Bonnie Woodin, Duffy Elementary School, Tucson, Arizona

Scientific Consultant:

Dr. Mark Dimmitt, Arizona-Sonora Desert Museum

Editorial Consultants:

Elizabeth Pennisi, freelance writer, Washington, D.C.
Rebecca Staples, Elizabeth Shaw Editorial Services, Tucson, Arizona

The producer wishes to thank Crown's Executive Editor Andrea Cascardi, who helped shape and strengthen the text, oversaw page design, and cheered us on, and Crown's former Editor-in-Chief David Allender, who saw potential for a desert book in the HIDDEN LIFE series, launched with Dwight Kuhn's photos. Tribute too goes to Dr. Thomas A. Wiewandt, whose previously published desert photos earned our invitation to participate in this series.

Text and photographs copyright © 1990 by Thomas A. Wiewandt

Series concept development and photo/editorial coordination by the Soderstrom Publishing Group Inc. and Dwight Kuhn, series editor.

Published by Crown Publishers, Inc., a Random House Company, 225 Park Avenue South, New York, New York 10003

CROWN is a trademark of Crown Publishers, Inc.

Manufactured in Japan

Book design by Kathleen Westray

Library of Congress Cataloging-in-Publication Data
Wiewandt, Thomas.
The hidden life of the desert / Thomas Wiewandt.   p.   cm.
Summary: Photographs and text give a guided tour of animals, plants, and ecology of the desert in America's Southwest.
ISBN 0-517-57355-5—ISBN 0-517-57356-3 (lib. bdg.)
1. Desert ecology—Southwest, New—Juvenile literature.   2. Desert ecology—Juvenile literature.   3. Desert ecology—Southwest, New.
[1. Desert animals.   2. Desert plants.]   I. Title.
QH104.5.S6W45   1990   89-22263
574.5'2652'0979—dc20   CIP
                                                         AC

10 9 8 7 6 5 4 3 2 1

First Edition

Sand verbenas and evening primroses

It has been a mild, wet winter in the warm desert of the American Southwest. Now in spring, like magic, millions of sweet-smelling flowers appear. Such a sight comes only once every 8 to 10 years. Just weeks after blooming, these delicate plants will wither and vanish in the hot, dry air. Their seeds must wait patiently for another wet year.

In deserts, all living things must stay in tune with rain, ready for its coming and prepared for its going. In the Sonoran Desert we find an exciting parade of plant and animal life. Creatures living here know five seasons of the year: spring, dry summer, wet summer, autumn, and winter. The spring and summer seasons are the busiest.

Every spring, the Sonoran Desert is a wonderland of flowering trees, shrubs, and cactuses. These tough plants can endure long periods of heat and dryness. Most can bloom every year because they store much food and water in their stems and roots. In the morning sun, big, beautiful blossoms open on the fat, juicy stems of prickly pears. And paloverde (pollo-VER-day) trees wear a veil of tiny golden flowers. The paloverde has very long roots that reach deep into the ground for water.

Paloverde tree

Prickly pear

Ocotillo in flower

Cane cholla cactus flower

Desert iguana

Warm spring days bring lizards above ground. Those that have stayed cool and asleep under rocks or within burrows all winter begin their search for food. For the desert iguana, having creosote bush flowers to eat is a joy of spring. But most lizards would rather hunt insects.

Before starting to hunt each morning, lizards sunbathe to warm up. Many of these cold-blooded animals try to keep their daytime body temperature about the same as ours. An overheated collared lizard on a hot rock lifts his toes to keep from burning them. He then dashes for the shade.

Collared lizard

Zebra-tailed lizard

Gila monster

Diamondback rattlesnake

Lizards use "body language" to defend feeding and mating territories. Male zebra-tailed lizards try to scare away intruders by looking as big and fierce as possible.

The Gila (HEE-la) monster is the only lizard in the United States with venom. It holds on with a vise-tight bite and chews venomous saliva into its prey. Few people are lucky enough to see one of these big, shy lizards in the wild.

In spring, other reptiles also become active. Rattlesnakes are well camouflaged, so watch your step. They strike quickly and inject venom through long, hollow fangs.

Rattlesnakes and Gila monsters flick their forked tongues to sniff the air for a scent of prey. Rattlesnakes often wait by rodent trails for a meal to come by. Gila monsters dig into rodent nests and steal the young.

Roadrunners

Lizards beware—even hunters may become the hunted. A roadrunner catches lizards for its chicks to eat. Insects, rodents, young birds, centipedes, and small snakes (even rattlesnakes!) are on the roadrunner's menu as well.

The sharp spines of cactus plants discourage animals from eating them. Here birds can find safe places to nest. Curve-billed thrashers build open, stick nests much like the roadrunner's. The cactus wren weaves a grass-covered nest that is used year-round.

Curve-billed thrasher

Cactus wren

The largest animals in North American deserts are mule deer and bighorn sheep. Both live in rocky areas. They can sniff out small pools of water, but much of their water comes from plants they eat.

Mule deer have big ears, like mules. Male mule deer (bucks) grow antlers, which fall off every winter and regrow the next year. Females (does) have no antlers.

Mule deer doe

Bighorn sheep ewe with lamb

Bighorn sheep ram

Male bighorn sheep (rams) have large, curved horns, which grow longer and thicker every year and never fall off. The female (ewe) has much shorter, thinner horns. In spring and summer, lambs are born.

Saguaro cactus in flower

Dry summer begins in May, when the giant saguaro (suh-WAH-row) cactus blooms. Its white, waxy flowers open at night. In early morning they look fresh but soon shrivel in the hot sun. The flowers produce juicy red fruit, a tasty treat for many desert dwellers, including people.

A saguaro cactus may grow taller than a four-story building (50 feet). These giant cactus "trees" become living apartment houses. Woodpeckers peck out nest cavities in the fat stems. Quickly the plant seals the wound with a corky covering that protects against water loss and infection. Each family of woodpeckers makes at least one new nest hole every year. And when they move out, other birds, such as elf owls, move in. The elf owl stands only five inches high—it is the smallest owl in the world. These tiny owls hunt for insects and scorpions at night.

Gila woodpecker

Saguaro cactus fruit

Elf owls

A large saguaro cactus weighs about six tons, more than a big elephant. This great weight is supported by a woody internal skeleton, which remains even after the plant dies and its soft parts have rotted away.

Saguaro cactus skeleton

Honeybees in cactus skeleton

Bark scorpion with young

Honeybees, scorpions, birds, and many other creatures make their homes in cactus skeletons. Bark scorpions hide under loose pieces of dead cactus during the day and hunt at night. They sting insects to paralyze them, which keeps their meal from running away!

Scorpions do not lay eggs. Baby scorpions are born, and at birth crawl onto their mother's back. She protects her young but does not feed them. After a week, these tiny scorpions start to hunt for insects.

13

When the air is hot and dry, the leaves of many plants turn yellow and drop off. A leaf-fall in dry summer protects desert plants from losing too much water through their leaves.

Animals move out of the sun and search for water. Desert cottontails and Gambel's quail drink daily if water is near.

Desert cottontail

Gambel's quail

Round-tailed ground squirrel

Black-tailed jackrabbit

Ground squirrels dig burrows that stay cool even when soil at the surface becomes painfully hot.

Jackrabbits don't use underground burrows. They dig shallow resting places in the shade under bushes. Their huge, thin ears help them keep cool. On clear, hot summer days, jackrabbits can radiate heat from their ears—blood flowing through them loses heat before it returns to the body.

Coyote

As the sun sets, the desert begins to cool. Many animals that have been hiding become active.

Grasshopper mouse howling

Coyotes begin their search for food after sundown. The fierce little grasshopper mouse might become a coyote's next meal. Like the coyote, this mouse howls to communicate with others of its kind. Its howl is more like a high-pitched scream— nearly beyond the range of human hearing. Also like the coyote, the grasshopper mouse is a hunter. Although most mice eat plants, this one prefers scorpions, lizards, and insects.

Grasshopper mouse attacking cactus beetle

At night, a long-nosed bat laps nectar from blossoms of the century plant. This sweet, energy-rich drink is fuel for the bat. And without knowing it, the bat helps the plant. Pollen that sticks to the bat's fur is carried from flower to flower and helps century plants produce seeds.

Long-nosed bat at century plant flowers

Kangaroo rat

Conenose bug

Like bats, many desert rodents are active at night. But one kind of rodent, the kangaroo rat, never needs to drink. From seeds and other dry foods it eats, this large jumping mouse makes water within its body and can use it again and again!

Rodent nests are breeding grounds for conenose bugs, also called kissing bugs. Like mosquitoes, these insects get food and water by sucking blood from larger animals. The insect's beak is so sharp that the bites can hardly be felt. Kissing bugs bite people, too. The swelling is often large and very itchy.

Just when time seems
to be standing still in the
summer heat, winds begin to
blow from the south . . . from
the seacoast of Mexico. The
wind brings moist air, and
clouds start to form.

As thunderstorms build
in late afternoon, the air
becomes charged with
electricity. Spectacular
lightning shows begin.

The summer wet season arrives in late June or early July with high winds and driving rains. The rain may be so heavy that it rushes down the hillsides before it can soak into the ground. Dry streambeds (arroyos) fill quickly. Each storm is brief—these flash floods normally last less than an hour.

For many desert creatures, summer's first flooding rain begins a new year. The rumble of thunder and the pounding of raindrops on the desert floor tell this spadefoot toad that it is time to wake up. Nature's alarm clock has awakened him from ten months of sleep underground!

Spadefoot toad

Male spadefoot toad calling

Male and female toads spawning

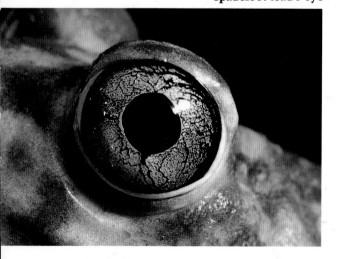

Spadefoot toad's eye

Male spadefoot toads hop to nearby rain puddles and call "eeeoow, eeeoow, eeeoow." This loud song attracts females. When a female comes close, the male grabs her tightly. The two then swim together—while she lays eggs, he releases a nearly invisible cloud of sperm into the water. His sperm fertilize the eggs, starting their growth.

This burst of activity continues all night. At sunrise, each toad leaves the water and hops off alone. Using their rear feet, spadefoots dig new holes, where they can safely sit and wait for another very wet night. Then they will hunt for insects. To make it through a year of sleep underground, spadefoots need only one big meal.

Spadefoot toad eggs

Spadefoot tadpoles and fairy shrimp

One spadefoot tadpole eating another

A spadefoot must develop from egg to tadpole to tiny toad before the puddle dries up. Spadefoot eggs can hatch in just one day. Swimming tadpoles eat enormous amounts of plant and animal foods. The more animal matter they eat, the faster they grow. A few spadefoot tadpoles grow larger than the others—these eat fairy shrimp, and some eat their smaller brothers and sisters!

A tadpole must grow lungs and legs before it can crawl onto dry land. Only then is it ready for life as a toad.

Tarantula

There are giants in the desert, with eight legs or more: 4-inch spiders, 6-inch millipedes, and 9-inch centipedes. Rain brings them above ground in search of food, water, and mates.

Huge hairy spiders called tarantulas seem scary but rarely bite people. Tarantulas help us by eating insect pests.

After summer storms, rainworms—giant desert millipedes—are sometimes seen crossing roads by the thousands. Millipedes eat plants, especially dead ones. As they grow, they add legs. Big rainworms have 250-300.

If attacked by a hungry animal, millipedes curl into a tight coil and release a nasty-tasting fluid through openings along the body.

Giant desert millipede

Giant centipede

The giant centipede is tastier to some birds and mammals, but it can move quickly. Smart predators should attack the head end first, to stop a centipede's painful biting. But which end is which? This confusing choice may give the centipede a chance to escape.

Collared peccaries

Collared peccary yawning

On cloudy, cooler days, some of the nighttime (nocturnal) animals, such as the collared peccary (PECK-uh-ree) and the kit fox, stay active. Peccaries, also called javelinas (hav-a-LEEN-ahs), are distant cousins of pigs. They travel in small family groups and are among the few animals that can eat cactus stems, spines and all.

The desert kit fox is the smallest fox in North America. It weighs less than the average house cat. Like other foxes and coyotes, it digs an underground den, hunts small animals, and eats wild fruits.

Desert kit fox

31.

Desert tortoise

In wet summer, when fruit of the prickly pear cactus ripen, animals have a feast. Desert tortoises eat so much fruit, their faces are stained purple. Tortoises are turtles that live on dry land. Like all turtles, tortoises never grow teeth. Instead, they have a sharp beak that cuts food.

Birds peck holes in cactus fruit to reach the sweet, juicy pulp inside. Then insects, such as the golden paper wasp, can eat the leftovers.

For the cactus mouse, moving just one cactus fruit is a struggle!

Golden paper wasp

Cactus mouse

Desert broom

Autumn is a dry time with sunny days and chilly nights, a time when seeds of the desert broom float away on the wind. Cactuses and most other desert plants stay green. But where mountains meet the desert floor, and where streams often flow, you find water-loving broadleaf trees such as sycamore, cottonwood, and ash. In autumn, their leaves turn yellow and orange and then fall off, just as in northern forests.

White-tailed deer

Leafy plants that grow along streams attract animals you won't see in the open desert. White-tailed deer come down from the mountains.

Elf owls are now flying south, to warmer places in Mexico. Tortoises are slowing down, as they dig deep into the ground. Desert animals are preparing for winter.

Bobcat

Snow is rare in this desert, a winter treat for people that is no treat for a cactus. In Arizona, many cactuses suffer from frostbite. Saguaros may live for 200 years here, but nighttime cold can kill them before they reach this age. Their juices protect them only against light freezes.

Reptiles, toads, and rainworms are now underground. Most are in deep sleep, barely living but healthy. Even mice have slowed down. Yet a few creatures carry on. Some, like bobcats, are well-dressed for the cold. Kangaroo rats are still busy gathering seeds, and jackrabbits are still outrunning coyotes. There's less chatter among quail now, as they peck at fresh winter greens.

Come March, winter's peace will be broken by a fiesta of new life, starting the cycle of seasons once again.

You have just visited the northern part of the Sonoran Desert, in Arizona and southern California. Here there are five seasons, including two summers, one dry and one wet. Scattered thunderstorms come in wet summer, with gentler rains in winter. But desert plants and animals never know exactly how much rain will fall. Lowlands at Tucson, Arizona, may get as little as 5 inches of rain or as much as 24 inches in different years. And only a half day's drive away—near the California border—people sometimes see less than 1 inch of rain in a year.

The biggest part of the Sonoran Desert lies in Mexico, where seasons and landscapes may differ from those in this book. For example, if you lived by the Pacific Ocean in Mexico's Baja California, you might see only three seasons and plenty of fog but very little rain.

Other desert lands in North America are colder. In Utah and Nevada freezing winter temperatures and dryness kill most cactuses and desert trees. So there you see miles and miles of small bushes and grasses.

About one third of all land in the world receives less than 15 inches of rain or snow each year. And more than half of this dry land is called *desert*—it normally receives less than 10 inches. A few deserts are so cold or so dry that almost no plants can grow. And in parts of others, soils are too thin, too sandy, or too salty for nearly all plants and animals.

Natural deserts can be beautiful. But today, deserts are growing unnaturally where plants have been stripped away for livestock, for firewood, or for other uses. Plants hold moisture and fertile soil. As plants vanish, the air becomes even drier, and deserts spread, some by as much as 30 miles a year. Man-made deserts are ugly and disastrous for people who must live in them. Even where water can be brought in, desert soils normally turn salty through farming, and salt kills most crops. Solutions to such problems are often expensive and temporary.

Wild plants and animals have learned to live within the limits of deserts. And so must we.